D1404793

Costume Designer

Helen Mason

Gareth Stevens
PUBLISHING

Please visit our website, **www.garethstevens.com**. For a free color catalog of all our high-quality books, call toll free 1-800-542-2595 or fax 1-877-542-2596.

Library of Congress Cataloging-in-Publication Data

Mason, Helen.
Costume designer / by Helen Mason.
p. cm. — (Creative careers)
Includes index.
ISBN 978-1-4824-1334-2 (pbk.)
ISBN 978-1-4824-1289-5 (6-pack)
ISBN 978-1-4824-1439-4 (library binding)
1. Costume design — Vocational guidance — Juvenile literature. 2. Costume design — Juvenile literature. I. Mason, Helen, 1950-. II. Title.
PN1995.9.S4 M37 2015
791.4302023—d23

First Edition

Published in 2015 by
Gareth Stevens Publishing
111 East 14th Street, Suite 349
New York, NY 10003

Developed and produced for Gareth Stevens Publishing by BlueApple*Works* Inc.
Editor: Marcia Abramson
Art Director: Melissa McClellan
Designer: Joshua Avramson

Photo Credits: Dreamstime: © Markwaters p.6; © Randy Miramontez p.8; © Steve Mann p. 11; © Radekdrewek p.12; © Breakers p. 14 top; © Lucy Cherniak p. 15; © Araraadt p. 15 right; © Denis Makarenko p. 18 top; © Ermess p. 18; © Batareykin p. 19 top; © Pavel Losevsky p. 19; © Photographerlondon p. 21; © Illustrart p. 30 top; © Vvoevale p. 31; © Lisa F. Young p. 32; © Joneil p. 33 left; © Carrienelson1 p. 40 bottom; © Abxyz p. 42 top; © Cancer741 p. 42 bottom; © Claudio Balducelli p. 44; © CBS/Photofest: p. 9; © Fox Searchlight Pictures/ Photofest p. 10; iStock: © VvoeVale p. 38 top, 39 left; Keystone Press: © Tracy Barbutes p. 13 left; © JM11 p. 9 right; © Gary Lee p. 41 top; © INB p. 41 bottom; Shutterstock: © testing cover, top left; © Fotomicar cover top right; © criben cover bottom left; © Melodia plus photos cover bottom right; © Elnur cover; © T-Design title p.; © Eduardo Rivero TOC backgound; © wavebreakmedia p. TOC, 27 p.; © Kzenon p.4; © Igor Bulgarin p. 5; © df028p.7; © justasc p. 14; © Sam Aronov p. 16 top; © Pukhov Konstantin p.16; © Andrey Malgin p. 17; © Ilya Rabkin p. 20; © Diego Cervo p. 22; © marekusz p.23; © Monkey Business Images p. 24, 44 top; © NatBasil p.25 top; © Northfoto p. 25; © lian_2011 p. 26 top; © borzywoj p. 28; © CandyBox Images p. 29; © Vietrov Dmytro p. 30; © Samuel Borges Photography p. 32 top; © sam100 p. 33 right; © DenisNata p. 34; © Africa Studio p. 35; © Dragon Images p. 36; © Igor Bulgarin p. 37; © yuri4u80 p. 38; © lanych p. 39 top; © vvoe p. 39 right; © silver tiger p. 39 bottom; © Natykach Nataliia p. 42 middle; © Nejron Photo p. 43 right; © ChameleonsEye p. 45; Public Domain: p. 8 top, 6, 40 top, 43 left; Wikkicommons: © Effie p. 12 top; © Bobak Ha'Eri p. 36 top; © atp_tyreseus p. 37 top

All rights reserved. No part of this book may be reproduced in any form without permission from the publisher, except by reviewer.

Manufactured in the United States of America

CPSIA compliance information: Batch #CS15GS. For further information contact Gareth Stevens, New York, New York at 1-800-542-2595.

Contents

What Is a Costume Designer?

Do you enjoy dressing up? Do you appreciate the color and texture of **fabrics**? Do you like to experiment with outfits? Do you love the performing arts? If you answered yes to any of these questions, you might make a terrific costume designer.

When you watch TV shows, movies, and plays, you are seeing the work of costume designers. These designers help to create not only the clothes the characters wear, but also the whole look and tone of the **production**.

Costume designers combine a love for costume with a flair for design. To get ideas, they study both today's styles and fashions from history. If they are designing costumes for a science fiction show, they imagine how people will dress in the future!

◄ The role of the costume designer is to create the characters' clothes and balance the scenes with texture and color.

Creativity Is the Key

Costume designers research what is needed for a film or program. They then design the costumes. The word "costume" refers to clothes, hats, shoes, and accessories, such as jewelry and canes. Costume designers make, buy, remake, and rent clothes and other **props** that make the characters in the story come to life. Their costumes show the occupation, social status, gender, age, and individuality of each character. They reinforce the mood and style of the production.

Did You Know?

The signature looks of popular shows often become fashion trends. Feather earrings and black-and-white-striped dresses appeared in stores after they were used in the TV show Pretty Little Liars.

▼ Costumes for this ballet version of Romeo and Juliet are based on styles of the 1590s, when Shakespeare wrote his famous play.

Types of Costume Designers

There are four main areas of costume design. Some designers work in all four, while others specialize in just one.

Historical Costume Designers

Historical costume designers develop costumes for a specific time period. They research clothing styles in libraries, **museums**, and on the Internet. For a play about the Middle Ages, for example, they would look at medieval paintings and statues to see what peasants and nobles wore. These designers work closely with historians and other experts in a particular time period.

Designers for Fantasy and Science Fiction

Designers for fantasy and science fiction can let their imagination run free. They make each character distinctive and memorable. Some of their sleek designs have inspired modern sportswear.

◄ Science fiction designers have created unforgettable costumes for famous movies, such as Star Wars.

Contemporary Costume Designers

How do designers make characters look contemporary? They study people on the street. They read magazines. If the performers don't look like regular people, they won't be able to connect with their audience.

Did You Know?

The **budget** for each contestant's outfit on American Idol is $400 per episode. Contestants get to keep the outfits they wear, which are often made by new designers who want their name on the show.

Dance Costume Designers

Creating costumes for dancers takes special skills. Costumes become a key part of the performance as dancers whirl across the stage. These costumes must be visually beautiful while also allowing the dancers to move freely. Designers research modern fabrics to help them improve dance costumes.

▼ Costumes for dancers must allow for a lot of body movement. That is why ballerinas traditionally wear short skirts, called tutus, over tights. Tutus can be made from many different materials—including feathers!

Costume Design for Television

Everyone who appears on television wears a costume, whether they are acting in a show or delivering the news.

Costume Planning

Costumes help to tell the story when you watch a TV show. Is the character young or old? Rich or poor? Good or bad? Designers must create clothes that are true to each character's personality. To do this, they need to understand how different fabrics and styles work for each actor in a show.

▲ *Actors film a scene for* Law & Order: Special Victims Unit. *Their costumes are based on what real detectives wear.*

▼ *The stars of* Glee *wear matching costumes in a scene from the show. Lou Eyrich, who designed costumes for the first three seasons, wanted them to look like a real high school glee club.*

Budgets and Continuity

Television costume designers read a script to look for clues about what a character might wear. If there's a related book, they often read that, too. If the show is historical, they research clothes of the time.

Many TV costumes are designed for a specific show. To save money, designers often shop in department stores and used clothing shops.

For both series and films, continuity is important. A character who runs to the kitchen and then returns with a snack must be wearing the same outfit, even though the scenes are shot on different days. The costume designer is responsible for checking this.

Did You Know?

Some costumes from TV shows have become so famous that they have been put on display at the National Museum of American History in Washington, DC.

▼ *Male characters in* The Big Bang Theory *wear geek outfits designed by Mary T. Quigley.*

Costume Design for Film

Film costume designers help to create the overall style of a movie. To make sure each character looks right in each scene, they have to become experts in making movies.

Keeping It All Together!

Film costume designers must communicate well. They make sure actors are comfortable in their costumes, explain any special features, and oversee **alterations**. If writers, directors, producers, and actors have their own ideas for costumes, the designer listens to them and works with them. The designer also must keep track of changes in the script and adapt costumes quickly.

▼ *Since there are few photographs of slaves available, Patricia Norris, the Oscar-nominated costume designer for* 12 Years a Slave, *relied on research and educated guesses to make the wardrobe look as real as possible.*

Design Work

Design work starts long before filming. Designers can work for months researching, planning, and supervising wardrobe development. They consider how movement and lighting might affect how a costume looks. Every detail has to be right. They also notice and fix any design problems, because the outfit may not flatter someone once they put it on.

Costume designers hire staff members who build, alter, and take care of costumes. Many designers negotiate their own contract and those for the people they hire.

Did You Know?

Before starting the costumes for The Hunger Games, Judianna Makovsky read the entire series. She researched the clothing worn by coal miners and fashions from both the 1930s and 1700s.

▼ Costume designer Julian Day works on the set of Rush, *a 2013 movie about rival auto racers in the 1970s. The costumes reproduced the racing suits used at that time, complete with fire safety equipment.*

Costume Design for the Theater

These costume designers design clothing for operas, musicals, and stage plays.

Before the Show

Theater costume designers must ensure that costumes reflect the story being told and show the characters' personalities accurately. Costume colors and fabrics must also consider bright stage lighting. In most cases, designers don't want their fabrics to create glare.

▲ *The mask for the* Phantom of the Opera *must be clearly visible but not hinder the actor's ability to see or speak.*

Some actors must change quickly between scenes. Designers consider this when making costumes. For quick changes, an actor may wear one costume under the other.

During and After the Show

Costume designers make sure all costumes are ready for the first dress rehearsal. During that rehearsal, they make sure everything works. They may fix any tears and make changes if something doesn't look right.

After the last show, they make sure costumes are removed from the theater. **Stock costumes** belong to the theater, and these are cleaned and stored. Rented and borrowed pieces are returned to their owners.

Did You Know?

Maria Björnson designed the glamorous costumes for The Phantom of the Opera. Over 20 years, this show played to more than 100 million people in 21 countries.

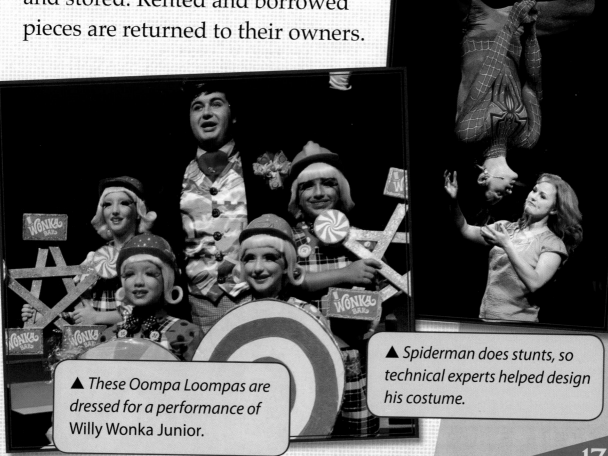

▲ These Oompa Loompas are dressed for a performance of Willy Wonka Junior.

▲ Spiderman does stunts, so technical experts helped design his costume.

13

Costume Design in Museums

Museum costume design varies depending on the type of museum.

History Museums

▲ New York's Metropolitan Museum of Art has more than 35,000 costumes.

Many history museums **exhibit** samples of clothing from the past. Some of these have been donated by the families of famous people. Other exhibits include clothing reproductions. This is clothing that has been made using fabrics and styles from the past. Women in an exhibit about the Civil War might wear reproductions of dresses with hoop skirts.

Many of these museums host **reenactments** where people dress in **period costumes** and play scenes from the past. The Americans in Wartime Museum in Virginia shows people dressed like American soldiers as it tells wartime stories.

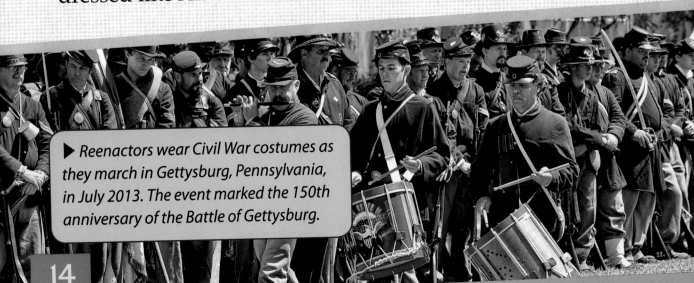

▶ Reenactors wear Civil War costumes as they march in Gettysburg, Pennsylvania, in July 2013. The event marked the 150th anniversary of the Battle of Gettysburg.

Other Museums

Art museums have costume design collections. In these museums, the costume designers serve as **curators**. They research materials for the collection, take care of the outfits, and keep background information on each item.

Children's museums and science centers can also include displays with costumed mannequins, or dummies. Some, such as The Children's Museum of Indianapolis, have a collection of clothes from other countries.

Did You Know?

New York's Irene Lewisohn Costume Reference Library has a collection of books, magazines, and clippings. It also has fashion prints, drawings, and photos.

▼ *A show in France featured elaborate theater costumes styled from the Baroque era of the 1600s.*

▼ *Many period costumes are needed for living history sites, such as the pioneer village pictured below.*

Costume Design Companies

Costume designers work for costume companies as designers, salespeople, and executives.

Costume Sales and Rental

Many costume companies have a large selection of ready-made and custom-made costumes for

▲ Costumes can make someone look like a famous star or a character from a popular movie.

sale or rent. They sell and rent costumes for film, theater, and television. These include period, ethnic, and career costumes, complete with wigs and hats. Some also carry trademarked costumes, such as official Batman and Barbie oufits. Others have military and police uniforms, complete with the correct **insignia** and medals.

▼ Police and army costumes must include the correct materials, colors, badges, and hats.

Other Markets

Many companies provide costumes to the public for special events, such as a carnival, **masquerade**, or other party. Some specialize in Halloween costumes for witches, pirates, vampires, and zombies. There are costumes for all ages, sizes—even pets! Many of these companies sell their costumes to stores as well.

Did You Know?

A gymnastics coach from Penn State University worked with a costume company to develop costumes with four-way stretch material. This material gives the skintight fit of modern outfits.

Other companies offer finding services. They search for hard-to-find items, such as gold buttons for a woman's dress from around 1900.

Still others specialize in dance costumes or sporting outfits. They work for local customers and many even supply international markets. Outfits for the 2012 Russian Olympic team in gymnastics were designed by an American costume company.

▶ Dance and skating costumes must cover and protect the performers' bodies. They must also focus attention on the performers.

Freelance Costume Design

Many costume designers work freelance. They go from project to project. Freelance designers may work for many different companies.

Variety of Work

Freelancers may design theater costumes for one project, then develop Halloween costumes for a costume company for the

▲ Outfits for a costume ball are often created by freelance costume designers.

next. One month they may work on a commercial. The next, they design the look for a music video. Freelance designers also develop a range of looks and styles. This includes contemporary, science fiction, and dramatic. Some specialize in dressing people for conventions and special social events.

▶ Commercials are another job for freelance costume designers. This one has a medieval theme.

Length of Job

Freelancers work long hours, including evenings and weekends. They usually focus on one job at a time and make sure the job stays on schedule. They often work during the preproduction phase. This is before filming or performing starts.

Usually, their job ends once production begins. On big-budget productions, the designer works throughout filming and performances.

Did You Know?

Joanna Johnston, the costume designer for War Horse, kept a picture of her great-uncle with her throughout filming. Her great uncle fought in World War I and was killed in France when he was 18.

▲ These scuffed boots show how much detail costume designers put into their work. Nothing must be overlooked.

▼ Music videos need costume designers, too.

Related Careers

Costume designers work all over the world, but production centers like Los Angeles and New York offer the most opportunities. Many shows are made in these two areas, so there are many jobs for people in these related careers.

Costume Buyer

Also called shoppers, costume buyers have an eye for fashion. They look for fabrics and clothing that follow the designer's vision. Buyers are used in productions with big budgets. Some do the purchasing for big-name actors who have a say about their wardrobe. They also work at theme parks and for costume companies.

▼ Costume buyers may search in vintage stores for clothes and inspiration for a movie or TV show set in the past.

Set Costume Supervisor

Set costume supervisors lead the costume department. They work with the designer to develop or assign costumes for each character. They make a list of characters and their costume needs for each scene. They organize costumes for each day of production. They also maintain costume continuity and manage the budget.

Did You Know?

Some productions have 1,000 or more costumes. On big-budget films, costume designers might work with a staff of 30 or more.

Costume Cutter

Costume cutters are also called fitters, drapers, or tailors. They make patterns for the clothes planned by the designer. They cut out and put together each garment. They do fittings and make alterations. They also care for all rented and pulled costumes. A pulled costume is one owned and stored by a performance company.

▶ This cutter marks the changes needed to this costume. The cutter will make alterations before the next fitting.

Day in the Life of a Costume Designer

The length of a costume designer's day depends on the project. Some days are spent in the office doing research, while other days are a whirlwind of shopping, fittings, and rehearsals. As the opening day of a production approaches, costume designers get busier and busier.

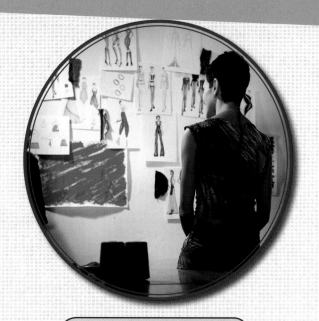

▲ *A costume designer studies her sketches.*

Research and Design Days

A research or design day may start with a team meeting at 9:00 a.m. The designer spends an hour with the director and the hair and makeup people as they brainstorm ideas for the next show or movie.

The designer and her research team head to the local library. Using books and online sources, they learn about the clothing styles of the time of the story.

In the early afternoon, the designer heads back to the office. She starts to "rough out" some ideas for one of the characters. For the rest of the working day, she reviews sample fabrics and chooses ones she thinks will be perfect for this character.

Production Days

Once production begins, costume designers are always on the go. Movies, plays, and TV shows have tight deadlines. The designer must make sure every costume is ready on time. This may require last-minute shopping for fabrics and props, then supervising cutters and tailors.

On other days, the designer supervises costume fittings at dress rehearsals. The designer may stay afterward to do repairs and make adjustments.

On filming days, designers are on the set early. This can mean getting up at 4:30 a.m. for a 6:00 a.m. shoot.

Did You Know?

Costume designers are often paid per production. Fees can range from $500 for a beginner to $20,000 for someone with experience. Top costume designers may make $150,000 for a single production.

▼ There's nothing like the feeling when an actor praises the costume a designer has spent so much time preparing.

The Work

The costume designer's job changes depending on the size of a production. In films and plays with large budgets, they create the idea and costume makers, wardrobe supervisors, and wardrobe assistants do the hands-on work. On smaller productions, costume designers do some or all of the hands-on work, too.

Research

Before they draw a single sketch, costume designers must decide which styles to use and how to create them. Designers get ideas from many sources, including websites, books, and museum collections. They may also discuss ideas with writers, actors, and directors. As their vision for the project comes together, costume designers use sketches and fabric samples to present their initial concepts.

▲ This design team discusses the design **roughs**. The director will have some suggestions. So will the people in makeup and lighting.

Travel

Costume designers usually work from an office or studio, but the job involves some travel, too. Designers need to see the production locations to check out the lighting and other conditions that may affect the look of the costumes. They also attend meetings with the production team.

▲ *Design roughs show the feel of a costume.*

Supervising

Costume designers supervise every aspect of the work. They write up schedules saying what needs to be done each day and who will do it. They make sure the cost stays within the project's budget. They arrange fittings for all cast members and make sure every costume is ready when needed.

▶ *Designers plan costumes for everyone in a film, even extras who appear briefly and have no lines.*

The Design Process

During the preproduction process, costume designers are given scripts to get an idea of how many characters are involved and what costumes are required. They then begin the complex task of developing costume plots for each character.

▲ **Undergarments** *affect the style and appearance of a dress. Bustles are frames or pads that enlarge the back of a woman's skirt.*

Read and Research

By reading the script carefully, the costume designer learns about the characters, plot, and setting. Next, the designer must learn the director's vision for the production. Sometimes the director has an unexpected idea, like setting a Shakespeare play in outer space. Whatever the concept, the designer now researches styles and fabrics for costumes.

▶ *Historic paintings and photos provide a lot of information about clothing of the past. This photograph is from the early 1920s.*

Collaborate

The costume designer is part of a team that includes the director, other production designers, and possibly the actors. As the next step, costume designers sketch costume ideas and discuss these with the rest of the team. They also develop a costume plot. This lists the characters in each scene and what they are wearing. Team members discuss their costume ideas and consider the roughs. Once people agree on an idea, the designer makes final sketches.

The finished designs, called finals, may include the newspaper clippings and copies of paintings used as references. The finals show the color scheme, swatches, hem lengths, and heel heights.

▼ *The chief director, lead actors, and the set, lighting, and makeup directors all have ideas about costume design.*

The Production Process

During the production process, the costumes are created using materials and fabrics that were decided on during the design process.

Prepare, Cut, and Sew

Depending on the costume, the fabric might need some adjustments. It may be dyed, beaded, or painted. Machine washing can give it a worn look if that is necessary for the character's appearance.

After the fabric has been chosen and prepared, a cutter makes a pattern from the design. The fabric is cut and the pieces are basted (roughly sewn) together with large stitches.

Some costumes start with a mock-up. This is a copy of the design made from inexpensive material. Design changes are drawn onto the mock-up and used to alter the pattern. The pattern is then used with the correct fabric.

▶ The pattern pieces are laid out on the fabric and then cut out.

Proper Fit

Each costume is built to fit the performer who wears it. This involves a number of fittings. At first, the costume is altered to fit the performer's body. If the costume requires special undergarments, such as a corset, an actor will wear them during the second fitting. Actors also wear shoes during fitting sessions to get the proper length of their costume.

Some costumes go to breakdown. Shoe polish, paint, sandpaper, cheese graters, and weights, for example, are used to make the costume look worn or aged.

During the dress rehearsal, actors wear their costume on stage for the first time. The designer makes notes about how it appears and may make minor changes.

Did You Know?

Corsets were used to make women fit into fashions from the 1500s to the 1900s. They had laces that were pulled tight to narrow the waist.

▼ After the pieces are basted together, a fitting is done to make final adjustments.

Tools Used

Costume designers use sketching tools, patterns, sewing tools, and measuring tapes.

Sewing Machines

Sergers are special sewing machines. As they sew, they cut off the edge of the material and wrap threads around the cut piece. This stops the material from fraying, so the costumes last longer than those made with regular sewing machines.

Sergers can use more than one spool of thread. This allows them to make special stitches used for decoration. They can also produce ruffles.

▲ Costume designers use both design and sewing equipment.

▼ This seamstress uses a serger to sew the seams of this costume.

Dummies

Dummies, or mannequins, provide an outline of the human body. The size of a mannequin is adjusted to suit the measurements of a performer. Clothes are first fit to the dummy, and then fitted to the actor.

Design Software

Today, many design roughs are done by hand. Designers use software to do the finals. Software programs have drawing capability. Most include a number of design templates or patterns a designer can customize for a specific time period or actor. Programs can add color, show the design in three dimensions, and even show fabric textures.

Digital Fashion Pro is a software that includes a mannequin the designer can dress in the design. This helps show what the clothing will look like when worn.

Did You Know?

A steamer removes wrinkles from clothes without ironing. Using distilled water lengthens the life of the steamer and keeps clothes from being stained by minerals found in tap water.

▼ Adjustable mannequins are used to make sure the costume fits the actor.

How to Become a Costume Designer

Now that you know more about it, are you interested in becoming a costume designer? Here are some ways to begin.

Start at Home

Practice creating different looks for yourself. Browse secondhand shops and pick up interesting items to make a costume or period look for a party. Also, experiment with different styles, colors, and textures.

▲ *Experiment with how different styles and colors affect your looks.*

Learn how to run a sewing machine and use your sewing skills to alter the look of an old outfit. You could consider changing the neckline of a dress you no longer wear or remaking an old pair of pants into capris. If you can, buy an inexpensive pair of jeans and experiment with different ways to make them appear worn.

◀ *Develop your sewing skills by making and altering your own clothes.*

Other Opportunities

Help with **amateur** theater costumes. Some amateur theaters have volunteers with professional training. Learn everything you can from them.

Work on student theater and film productions. Many of these are led by instructors with a background in the field. Listen to their suggestions and play around with different ideas and looks. It will help you get a feel for the different types of design.

When you are older, apply to work as a costume daily (a helper on a TV or film set).

Did You Know?

A little black dress is a simply cut dress that shows off the figure of the wearer. Audrey Hepburn is famous for the one she wore in the opening scene of the 1961 movie Breakfast at Tiffany's. The dress was designed by Givenchy, a French designer. Hepburn believed that "the costume designer makes the actor."

▲ Go to vintage clothing shops for inexpensive inspiration.

▲ Design Halloween costumes for yourself and friends.

33

Education

Becoming a costume designer requires education and training.

High School

The following high school courses will help prepare you for a career in costume design.

▲ *Many skills learned in art class can be transferred to costume design.*

- English and history teach research skills.
- Art provides information about texture, color, and design. It also gives experience sketching and using watercolors.
- Sewing classes teach basic measuring and stitching skills.
- Computer courses provide experience with various kinds of software.
- Marketing courses give training in budgeting and advertising.

Check what courses are needed for the university program you want to study. Make sure that you get those credits.

After High School

Most costume designers study art or design, and many get degrees in costume design, fashion, theater design, or performing arts as well. Some study millinery, or women's hats. Others attend fashion college.

Did You Know?

Costume design involves long working days. To meet deadlines, many designers work both evenings and weekends.

The other route is to start out as a wardrobe assistant or costume maker. Learn everything you can by observing and asking questions. By building contacts and gaining experience, you may be able to work your way up to costume design.

Some people **apprentice** in film and TV. An apprenticeship introduces young designers to the field. It provides them with hands-on experience as they work with knowledgeable costume designers.

▼ This design apprentice prepares costumes for the day's filming.

Costume Design Schools

Many schools teach costume design. Here are four that are well-known.

California Institute of the Arts

California Institute of the Arts (CalArts) offers both a BFA and MFA costume design program. The program emphasizes developing a personal design vision and the skills necessary for professional work.

▲ Students take part in theatrical work, films, dances, opera, and installations.

Fashion Institute of Design and Merchandising

A private college in California, the Fashion Institute of Design and Merchandising offers courses in both theater costume design and film and TV costume design, along with other fashion-related classes.

◄ This student gets coaching from an experienced costume designer.

Los Angeles City College

Los Angeles City College offers a certificate program in Costume Design. It has classes in design for theater, film, and television. It is a hands-on, practical course with lab time to learn skills as well as gain experience by working on student theatrical performances.

Tisch School of the Arts

The Tisch School of the Arts, part of New York University, has a graduate program called Design for Stage and Film. The department offers programs in Scenic Design, Production Design, Lighting Design, and Costume Design. These programs are for students who already have a college degree. Classes range from cutting and draping to stagecraft and opera.

▲ Tisch School of the Arts is in New York City, where design students can see many shows and sometimes work on them.

▼ Design students learn by doing costumes for all kinds of student plays.

Portfolio

You will need a **portfolio** of your designs to get into most college courses. You also will need one when applying for apprenticeship programs or a job.

What to Include

In your portfolio, include photos, drawings, and sketches of your costume work. Show all details, including color, and add fabric swatches. These will show the texture and feel of the design.

Label everything with the production name, your name, and the character name. Include the title of the play, TV show, movie, or other production. Use one or two designs per page, and of course, choose samples of your best work.

▲ Include preliminary sketches as well as final sketches.

◀ Character studies, which show all of a single character's costumes, should be part of a portfolio.

Quality

Invest in a high quality portfolio book. Make sure that it opens and lies flat so that several people can look at it at the same time.

All photographs in the portfolio should be in focus and of good quality. The order of pictures is important. If you have done a variety of work, organize it in themes. No matter the order, make sure that the last design is something recent and really good.

Update your portfolio as you get more experience.

Did You Know?

Most costume design programs require prospective students to submit portfolio materials online and bring portfolio materials to an in-person interview.

▲ Photograph the costumes you design on a simple background.

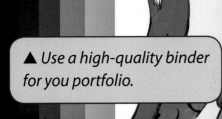

▲ Use a high-quality binder for you portfolio.

Learning from the Masters

Students of costume design learn from famous designers, including these four.

Bill Thomas

Bill Thomas (1920–2000) designed the costumes for more than 300 films. He was known for being able to design for any time period, whether historical or high fashion.

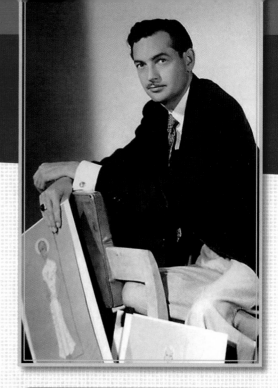

▲ *American designer Bill Thomas won an Oscar for the 1960 movie* Spartacus.

▲ *In 2012, Minnesota-born Lou Eyrich was awarded a Career Achievement Award from the Costume Designers Guild.*

Lou Eyrich

Lou Eyrich has won many honors for her costumes for TV shows, especially *Glee*. When she was in high school, she made costumes for her own glee club! Now she is one of the most influential costume designers working in TV and movies.

Mark Bridges

Born in Niagara Falls, New York, Mark Bridges studied costume design at the Tisch School of the Arts. He has designed the outfits for many movies and won an Academy Award for his work on *The Artist*. Bridges reveals character through texture, such as using sequins and beads to show Hollywood glamour.

▲ As a child, Mark Bridges loved movies, fabric, clothes, and color.

Sandy Powell

Born in London, England, in 1960, Sandy Powell learned from her mother how to sew. She is famous for the research she does to make sure that historical costumes are accurate. She thinks it's important to break down costumes by adding wear and dirt if that's part of the character or action.

▲ Sandy Powell has won three Oscars. Like Bill Thomas, she has been nominated 10 times for an Academy Award.

41

How Costume Design Evolved

Early costumes were masks. Costume design as we know it did not start until the 1800s.

Greek Plays

Dionysus was the Greek god of grapes and wine. Festivals in his honor led to the development of theater. Male actors played all the roles in Ancient Greece.

▲ A bust of the Greek god Dionysus.

They used masks to show which characters were female. Theaters were large, but there were no microphones or binoculars, so they also used masks to portray emotions. These masks—one smiling and one frowning—became a universal symbol for theater that is still used today.

▼ People in Ancient Greece watched theater plays in sloped, open-air arenas called amphitheaters.

Early Costumes

During the 1500s, actors wore the best clothes they could afford onstage. Costume was becoming a very important element of the performance. By the 1700s, actors competed to have the fanciest outfit.

By the 1800s, people started to pay attention to historical accuracy. Actors and set managers researched how people dressed during certain periods. Books with this information were published. By the beginning of the 1900s, most theaters used costume designers, even for contemporary plays.

Did You Know?

At first, all actors were male. Young boys played female parts. In 1662, King Charles II of England decreed that female roles should be played by females. The first actresses soon appeared onstage.

▼ This German costume book shows how men and women dressed in the 1800s.

▲ During the Elizabethan era, each of the colors used in costumes had its own meaning, which the audience understood.

You Can Be a Costume Designer

Do you still want to be a costume designer? Check out the following characteristics. Which traits do you have? Which ones are you developing?

▲ Sculpture classes teach about the human form.

I am

☐ interested in costume history
☐ able to put people at ease
☐ flexible
☐ ambitious

I enjoy

☐ imagining unique outfits
☐ fashion
☐ working with textures and colors
☐ working with people

If you have or are developing these traits, you might make a great costume designer.

▼ Community theater is a good place to learn about costume design.

Set Your Goal

Research the community and children's theaters in your area and volunteer to work with the costume department. Help to put together costumes for several plays. Offer to attend all rehearsals and performances. Help the actors dress and make sure that they have the props they need.

▲ *Seeing plays on Broadway in New York City will help you get design ideas. Many of the shows go on tour to other cities as well.*

Another great way to get involved in the costume design process is by working with your friends or community groups to plan and create costumes for local parades, such as the Santa Claus or Independence Day Parades.

Take pictures of the costumes you help create and sketch the parts that you developed. Make sure you store the photos and sketches in a notebook or costume design folder. As you get experience, start posting them online. There are plenty of free spaces to do this, including Facebook, Pinterest, Tumblr, and MySpace.

Glossary

alterations the process or result of changing something, often clothing

amateur a word to describe something done for fun, not as a job, or the person who is doing so

apprentice a person who learns a job or skill by working for a fixed period of time for a professional in a certain field

budget the amount of money available for spending on something, or a plan for how and when money will be spent

curator a person in charge of a group of things at a museum

exhibit a collection of items on display for public viewing

fabric a woven or knitted material, such as cotton or denim

insignia a badge or a sign indicating military rank or membership in a group

masquerade a party at which people wear masks and costumes

period costume clothing that re-creates what people wore in a historical era

portfolio a set of drawings, paintings, or photos that are presented together in a folder, or the folder itself

production the act or result of making something, often used for a play, movie, or TV show

prop an object that is used by the characters or seen in a movie, play, or TV show

reenactment an event that re-creates actions or a time period from history

roughs a drawing, often done by hand, showing the costume's feel

stock costume clothing that is ready to use to portray a common character, such as a witch

undergarment an old-fashioned name for underwear

For More Information

Books

LaMotte, Richard. *Costume Design 101: The Business and Art of Creating Costumes for Film and Television*. Studio City, CA: Michael Wiese Productions, 2001.

Leventon, Melissa. *What People Wore When: A Complete Illustrated History of Costume from Ancient Times to the Nineteenth Century for Every Level of Society*. New York, NY: St. Martin's Griffin, 2008.

Websites

Costume Designers Guild
www.costumedesignersguild.com
This group represents costume designers, assistant costume designers, and costume illustrators. Keep up to date with industry news and events.

BBC Design Trainee Scheme
www.bbc.co.uk/design/the_scheme.shtml
Find out about the BBC's trainee program.

The Costumer's Guide to Movie Costumes
www.costumersguide.com
Learn more about the costumes in some of the best-known movies.

Publisher's note to educators and parents: Our editors have carefully reviewed these websites to ensure that they are suitable for students. Many websites change frequently, however, and we cannot guarantee that a site's future contents will continue to meet our high standards of quality and educational value. Be advised that students should be closely supervised whenever they access the Internet.

Index